The Fast and Easy Guide to Networking for Introverts

How to Connect Without Going to Events, Making Cold Calls, or Sending Spammy Emails

GREG ROCHE

Copyright © 2020 Greg Roche

The Fast and Easy Guide to Networking for Introverts

Published by
King Rock, LLC. Littleton, CO

www.gregsroche.com

All rights reserved. No portion of this book may be reproduced in any form without permission from the publisher, except as permitted by U.S. copyright law.

For permissions contact:
greg@gregsroche.com

Cover by Shena Honey Pulido
Author photo by Mel Hill

ISBN: 9798693300545

To Sarah

Thanks for holding the string this time.

CONTENTS

HOW IT ALL STARTED	1
CHAPTER 1 – THE BUNDLE OF STICKS	9
CHAPTER 2 – THE ANT AND THE GRASSHOPPER	23
CHAPTER 3 – THE LION AND THE MOUSE	34
CHAPTER 4 – THE CROW AND THE PITCHER	45
CHAPTER 5 – THE MISER AND HIS GOLD	54
CHAPTER 6 – THE HARE WHO HAD MANY FRIENDS	64
CHAPTER 7 – THE HARE AND THE TORTOISE	75
CONCLUSION	83

HOW IT ALL STARTED

"I'm making some changes to the department. I'm eliminating your position."

Those were the words that came out of my boss's mouth after she sat down in my office on the afternoon of October 9, 2012. I was a vice president of human resources at a multifamily real estate company in Denver, Colorado.

I started at the company nine years earlier and worked my way up from an independent contract position in operations to one step below the head of human resources.

During those years, I focused on my work. I explored other job opportunities when recruiters had called me, but I never thought about what I would do if I suddenly lost my job.

Without warning, I needed to find a new job. I had a resume. That was it. I had no leads and, more importantly, no network.

We talk about networks in terms of things we build, comparing them to computer networks with nodes and connections. I prefer to think of my professional network as a garden.

Each conversation I have with someone is a seed. If I create a relationship with a person, I'm taking care of the seed. In time, it grows.

When I plant the seed, I'm not sure whether it will bear fruit or not, but I know if I don't care for it, it certainly won't grow. To grow your network, you need to plant a lot of seeds.

My networking garden started with people I knew. For me, most of them were people I worked with before.

As I talked to them, I realized there was a source of networking seeds I hadn't really thought of: company alumni or people who had worked with me at the same company.

When I started writing down a list of the people I had worked with over the past nine years, I was shocked. The list was much longer than I expected.

I used LinkedIn to look for people who had my former company's name in their profile. The list got longer. I had forgotten about a few people, but when I saw the LinkedIn search results, I thought, *Oh yeah! I remember him. I remember her.*

I had more networking seeds than I realized.

I have a confession.

I'm an introvert.

The thought of cold calling someone and asking them for help gives me heart palpitations. I would literally rather have major dental work than strike up a conversation with a stranger. Even when I try, my brain starts thinking of my opening line, and an argument breaks out between the side of my brain that wants to meet new people and the side of my brain that is scared of talking to new people.

"People talk to each other all the time, just say, 'Hello' and start the conversation," says the meet-new-people side of my brain.

"Are you nuts? What if we stutter and stammer and look like an idiot? We can't talk to new people, ever," says the scared-of-talking-to-new-people side.

This debate goes on in my head until the person I was going to talk to walks away or starts talking to someone else.

This is why I refuse to go to networking events. When I would go to conferences, I would usually spend most of the day standing in the corner trying to think of a way to strike up a conversation. At some of these conferences, I was a speaker! As a speaker, you have an automatic icebreaker with new people. "How are you enjoying the speakers at this conference?" Yet, I've always struggled to strike up a conversation.

But when I thought of the people I worked

with before, it wasn't scary to send them a simple email saying, "How have you been? I wanted to let you know I moved on from my last job, and I would love to talk to you about what you are doing now."

This was the first step in cultivating my networking garden. Some of these emails and LinkedIn messages were never answered. These seeds never sprouted, but many of them did, and I started to grow professional relationships with people who I hadn't talked to in years. Several of those seeds grew into plants and started to bear fruit.

One day in January 2013, a former colleague of mine sent me an email saying, "Hey, have you seen this job? It sounds like it might be right for you." He knew I was looking for a job because we had met for lunch. We had lunch because I had sent him an email asking to go to lunch. No secret networking technique here. Just a simple email to someone I knew. It was one of many that I sent. One of the many seeds I had planted.

I looked at the job my colleague had sent me, and I applied for it online.

This is where a lot of people stop in their job search process. They send in their application and never hear anything else about the job. Their application goes into the black hole of the applicant tracking system.

If you want to get a job, you have to mobilize

every tool available to you. In my case, the company I applied to was a health-care company. I thought of all the people in my networking garden who were in the health-care industry and asked them if they knew anyone at this particular company.

One man, a family acquaintance, knew the chief medical officer (CMO). I wasn't applying for a medical-related position, but I knew anyone with "Chief" in his job title was a good person to know.

My acquaintance sent an email telling the CMO I had applied for this job and asked who he could put me in touch with. Within a couple of days, I was contacted by a recruiter for an interview. The CMO had passed my name and contact information to the recruiting team.

When an executive sends your resume to recruiting, they call you for an interview. It's a professional courtesy. It's your ticket to the club. It gets you past the velvet rope, but once you get on the floor, it's up to you to dance. I had my shot at an interview, and it was time to shine!

I'll spare you the other parts of the interviewing process, except this one:

During my interview, my future boss asked which vendors I'd worked with at my other jobs. I gave her the names of the people and the companies I had worked with in the past. I went home after the interview and immediately received an email from one of those vendors saying the company I was interviewing with had called him asking about me. We had a good relationship, and he knew I was interviewing, so he was happy to give me a good recommendation.

I got the job!

And none of it was the result of going to networking events, making cold calls, or sending spammy emails.

One friend sent me the job posting.

One acquaintance passed my resume along to the CMO.

One vendor gave me a good recommendation.

I got the job because I had cultivated my networking garden.

What I learned from this experience:

- It's easy to go to work and do your job.
- It's easy to focus on the projects you are working on and forget about your networking garden.
- People only focus on the first two bullet points.

At the same time, you never know when your boss is going to walk into your office and tell you the department is changing, and your position has been eliminated. Maybe the company is merging with another company, and the headquarters are moving to another state. Maybe the company isn't doing well financially, and layoffs are coming. Maybe the entire economy is crashing, and your company is going bankrupt.

If any one of these things happen and your networking garden isn't already planted, putting the seeds in the ground at that time means it will take some time for them to grow and bear fruit.

I promised myself I would never be in that position again. I wasn't going to allow my networking garden to lay fallow.

In the years following my layoff, I continued to network. I'd send a few emails a week to former colleagues and people I knew. I'd look for people who were in the same industry and job title and contact them. I looked for ways I could connect with more people.

The more I connected, the more I learned about opportunities no one else knew about. I learned about people who were doing interesting things. People approached me asking for help.

I started sharing my networking approach with other people. I wrote articles on LinkedIn and guest posts on other people's websites about my approach to networking. I realized there were people out there, mostly introverts like me, who knew they needed to grow a professional network but didn't know how.

Like me, they hated the idea of going to networking events. The idea of cold calling and sending spammy emails to people they didn't know made their skin crawl.

I created webinars explaining how I grew my network. I started coaching groups of people who needed help. The introverts in my groups started growing their networking gardens and found success. They found new jobs and clients.

This book was written to share my networking approach with more people.

Each chapter starts with one of Aesop's fables.[1] I chose fables because they contain universal wisdom that has survived the test of time. Their lessons are memorable and applicable to different aspects of our lives, in this case to professional networking. I've merged what I've learned from my own experience and the experiences of my students with the lessons in these fables. Where I've included stories of my students, I've changed their names to preserve their privacy.

By tying my knowledge and experiences in professional networking to these timeless stories, I hope to teach you a different approach to networking that works especially well for introverts.

---

[1] Aesop, *Aesop's Fables* (Houston: Project Gutenberg, 1992)

CHAPTER 1 – THE BUNDLE OF STICKS

An old man on the point of death summoned his sons around him to give them some parting advice. He ordered his servants to bring in a bundle of sticks and said to his eldest son: "Break it." The son strained and strained, but with all his efforts was unable to break the bundle. The other sons also tried, but none of them was successful. "Untie the bundle," said the father, "and each of you take a stick." When they had done so, he called out to them: "Now, break," and each stick was easily broken. "You see my meaning," said their father.

Union gives strength.

We are stronger together. We are better together.

It's easy to think we don't need other people.

It's easy to think, *I'm self-sufficient. If I focus on being the best I can be, I won't need other people's help.* Some people don't want to ask for help. They believe it makes them appear weak.

But as the fable tells us, we are stronger together. Uniting your strengths with another person's strengths makes both of you stronger.

Right now, there is a group of people with whom you have professional relationships. You know them, and they know you. You help them, and they help you. At the same time, there are so many other people in the world you haven't met yet. You can't possibly meet every person who could help you in your career and in your life. There isn't enough time.

However, the people you already know have their own networks of people. Each person you know also knows a whole network of other people. Your network combined with the network of every person in your network opens up a whole world of new connections for you.

That's the value of a vibrant professional network. It allows you to leverage other people's professional relationships to connect you with opportunities you otherwise might not have.

Every time you grow a strong professional relationship with someone, you add his or her network to your network. You make her connections your connections and vice versa. As your network grows in professional relationships, it gets stronger.

What Is "Networking?"

When I start a new group coaching program, I ask everyone to tell me the first thing that pops into their minds when I say the word "networking." Usually, they tell me something like:

- Meeting new people at networking events.
- Exchanging business cards.
- Finding a job.
- It's awkward.
- It's salesy and sleazy.

Most people don't like to network. In 2014, Francesca Gino and a group of researchers from the Harvard Business School released a study called, "The Contaminating Effects of Building Instrumental Ties: How Networking Can Make Us Feel Dirty."[2]

The participants were given the task of turning word fragments into meaningful words using the first word that came to mind. The researchers provided participants with word

---

[2] Tiziana Casciaro, Francesca Gino, and Maryam Kouchaki, *The Contaminating Effects of Building Instrumental Ties: How Networking Can Make Us Feel Dirty* (Boston: Harvard Business School, 2014), 17-19.

fragments, such as W _ _ H, S H _ _ E R, and S _ _ P. These fragments could be completed as cleansing-related words (wash, shower, and soap) or as unrelated, neutral words (e.g., wish, shaker, and step).

The participants who completed the task after describing their networking experiences in detail most often completed the fragments with cleansing words. This led the researchers to conclude most people associate professional networking with feelings of uncleanliness. Even though the thought of networking makes people feel unclean, we've been told it's important to career and life success.

But why is it important? How does it make us stronger like the bundle of sticks in the fable?

Let's start with my definition of networking:

Creating professional relationships with people you know and trust for mutual benefit.

Notice, I called them "professional relationships."

I'm going to use terms like "network" and "connections" in this book. These words may sound cold or sterile, but the fact is, I'm not going to talk about friendships. I'm not talking about people you want to spend your free time with on weekends. Professional relationships are people you want to work and do business with.

Also, my view of networking is about mutual benefit. This isn't about what's in it for me. It's true I advocate networking to advance your career or business, but not at another person's expense. Each professional relationship should be viewed as a two-way street. You should pursue networking with the mindset of what you can give to other people.

Everyone has different goals. Some people are trying to establish themselves in a career. Some people are trying to build their own businesses. Everyone is looking for opportunities.

No matter what opportunities you're looking for, networking helps you find them. At the same time, networking is not going to turn those opportunities into a job or a new client. That's up to you and your skills and experience. You can't just meet a person and expect them to give you whatever you ask for. You need to show up. Networking helps you figure out where to show up. Networking gets you the audience.

There are a few more beliefs I have about networking:

- It's a skill that requires intentional practice.
- It doesn't come naturally to people, especially introverts.
- There's a lot of inaccurate information in

the world about networking.
- Most people have the wrong impression of networking, and that's the reason they don't do it.
- Learning how to network will improve your life, no matter what you do for a living.

The last belief, that networking will improve your life, is one most people don't understand. When I talk to people about networking, they say, "I'm not looking for a job right now." They only think about networking when they need to find a job.

But there are three reasons you need to grow your professional network, even if you aren't searching for a new job:

- Knowledge and authority
- Talent
- Career insurance

Knowledge and Authority

You can acquire knowledge in different ways. You can read about it, you can go to class to learn about it, or you can get it from firsthand experience.

Another very efficient way is to acquire it from other people's experiences. You can get it from people who have already solved the problems you're facing. Find out who has solved the problem and ask for advice.

Sounds simple, right?

However, most people aren't sitting around like a guru on the mountaintop waiting for you to come to ask them for advice. Even if they were, would you know how to find them?

Networking allows you to find people who already have the answers or at least the experience to help you gain the knowledge you need to do your job better or to solve a problem you're working on. If the person you need to talk to isn't already connected to you, they're less likely to help you. Who are you, and why should they give you their knowledge?

Having a professional connection with them will make them more likely to share their knowledge with you.

Let's look at this from the other side, the side where you are the one with the knowledge or the authority on a subject. Even if you aren't looking for a new job, you want to make yourself someone people value. But you can't stand on the corner and shout your advice to people. I mean, you can, but people will mistake you for a mentally unstable person and likely cross the street to avoid walking past you.

For people to trust your knowledge and advice, they need to get to know you. You want to grow professional relationships so that you become the go-to resource in your area of expertise. You already have a lot of experiences that are valuable to other people. You have perspectives people will want and need.

What's your authority? What special knowledge do you have that you could share?

When people already know you and what you can do, they invite you to work with them. You get opportunities you wouldn't get if you simply kept your knowledge and authority to yourself.

I've had the opportunity to give guest lectures at a university about the topic of professional networking. The opportunity came to me through my professional network. The professor of the class and I met and established a professional relationship. I met her before she started teaching at the university. We get together periodically and talk about what we're working on, and I was able to share my ideas on networking.

Since she knows me and knows what I talk about, she asked me to come talk to her business communications class. This worked well for her because she didn't have to spend hours finding someone to talk to her class about this topic. She knew me and knew I had knowledge and authority on the topic. She invited me to present to her class. It worked well for me because it gave me an opportunity to share what I know with her students and the other faculty.

Who knows where this opportunity will lead, but it all started because I was able to share what I do with one of my networking connections who came to know and trust me as an authority on this topic.

Talent

Besides figuring out who has the answers to questions, you can also identify people who would be talented individuals you'd like to work with on your team or in your business.

I was connected with an HR leader in Denver, and during a morning coffee meeting, she said to me, "Our company has a talent imperative." I hadn't heard this statement before, so I pressed her for more information. She said, "All executives are asked to network and meet talent that could someday join our company. I'm not recruiting you today, but someday, I might have a role you would be great for, and I want to be connected with you already."

If you lead a team or are part of a team in your organization, you can create your own "talent imperative" to begin meeting people who you might want to hire someday. When you are able to recommend top talent to your organization because you already have a professional relationship with them, your value in the organization is going to skyrocket.

To locate this talent and persuade them to join your team, you're going to need to get to know them first. You're going to need to establish a professional relationship with them. While you may present a talented person with an employment opportunity, this person needs to know you're legitimate and a person he or she would want to work for.

By networking with talent before you have an opportunity for them, you'll be able to quickly contact them and start the process of bringing them into your organization.

Career Insurance

Do you have a career insurance policy?

Bad things happen. Cars crash. Houses burn. People get sick. Sometimes they die. All of these things have financial consequences. In most cases, people don't have enough cash in the bank to pay for these consequences. But everyone knows these things could happen. To protect themselves, people buy insurance.

Insurance exists to reimburse you if something bad happens. If you die early, your life insurance policy helps your family financially. If you get hurt and can't work, disability insurance helps with your bills until you get better. If your house burns down, your homeowner's policy gets you a new house. If your car is in an accident, auto insurance pays to have it repaired.

Losing your job is a bad thing. In the US, when you have a job, your employer pays for unemployment insurance. If you lose your job involuntarily, you can qualify for unemployment payments. These payments are intended to replace some of your income while you look for another job, but that's not enough for people to maintain their current standard of living. For most people, their job is the single biggest, and likely only, source of income. Most people don't have enough cash in the bank to pay the bills if they don't have a job.

There's no insurance policy you can buy that would replace all of your income if you lost your job. But there is a way to insure your income in the event you lose your job. You can't get this policy from a broker or insurance company. You must create this policy yourself.

Your Professional Network Is Your Career Insurance Policy

It's the quickest way to find your next job.

How prepared are you for the sudden loss of your biggest source of income? Do you have a professional network that could quickly notify you of potential career opportunities? Would your network know what you are currently working on, what your skills are, and how you have created value for your employer?

Would your professional network be willing to refer you to their connections or would they think to themselves, *I haven't heard from this person in years, and he's suddenly contacting me because he needs a job?*

How do you create a career insurance policy? Grow a vibrant professional network.

Let's go back to the bundle of sticks in the fable.

It's easy to imagine all of the sticks are the same size in length and width. But if you went outside and picked up a bundle of sticks, some would be longer, and some would be shorter. Some would be thick, and others would be thin. Some would be green, having just fallen off the tree, and some would be brittle, having been on the ground for a while.

As you grow your professional network, you will be connecting with different types of people. Some people will have a large network of professional connections, and others will be starting out with their networking efforts. Some people will have professional status as the leader of an organization, and others will be starting their first job. As individuals, they may be strong or weak sticks.

No matter what the individual people look like, when you tie them together, they will be difficult, if not impossible, to break. If you had only one connection, you would still be stronger together than separately. If you added one more connection, then the three of you would be stronger than two of you. Each relationship you add, adds strength.

You need to continue to stay close to your

connections. You don't need to talk to your professional connections every day, but you need to keep them close to you — metaphorically speaking. If you make a connection once and then don't talk to them for a while, they aren't part of your bundle. Just like a weak tie around the bundles of sticks would allow the sticks to fall apart, your network needs to stay connected over time to maintain its strength.

Networking isn't about connecting one time. It's about growing relationships. It is about creating professional bonds. These bonds form over time through consistent connection.

Now that you know why you need to grow your "bundle" of professional connections, what's next?

Think about these questions and write down the answers:

- What is one thing you would like to learn about? Who do you know that already knows this?
- Do you have a business, or do you work at a company? Who from your career or life would you like to add to your dream team? Who are people you could talk to about joining you?
- If you lost your job today, other than friends and family, who would be the first person you would call to ask for advice?

The purpose of these questions is to start thinking about who you can connect with. You may be able to come up with anywhere from one to one hundred people to connect with. For now, I'd encourage you to simply come up with one person.

As you think about growing your vibrant professional network, remember the fable about the bundle of sticks, and remember this saying:

"If you want to go quickly, go alone. If you want to go far, go together."
—African proverb

CHAPTER 2 — THE ANT AND THE GRASSHOPPER

In a field one summer's day, a Grasshopper was hopping about, chirping and singing to its heart's content. An Ant passed by, bearing along with great toil an ear of corn he was taking to the nest.

"Why not come and chat with me," said the Grasshopper, "instead of toiling and moiling in that way?"

"I am helping to lay up food for the winter," said the Ant, "and recommend you to do the same."

"Why bother about winter?" said the Grasshopper. "We have got plenty of food at present." But the Ant went on its way and continued its toil. When the winter came the Grasshopper had no food and found itself dying of hunger, while it saw the ants distributing every day corn and grain from the stores they had collected in the summer.

Then the Grasshopper knew:

It is best to prepare for the days of necessity.

In 2007, things were going well in the United States:

- Unemployment was under 5%.
- Housing prices were hitting highs.
- The stock market was hitting levels that had never been seen before.

If you were an ant during this time, you knew the best thing you could do was make sure you weren't overleveraged on your house, add to your savings account, and outperform your colleagues at work.

Even though you weren't looking for a new job, you were cultivating your professional network. You spent a few minutes each day planting seeds by reaching out to old colleagues and friends. You watered those seeds by turning emails and phone calls into coffee or lunch meetings. Those informal, friendly conversations with your current network of connections bloomed and put you in touch with new people.

You learned which companies were doing

exciting new things. You met the people in your industry who were difference makers and willing to help you. You weren't asking them for anything, but you were sharing your thoughts and ideas. Your professional network was expanding with small amounts of effort every week.

Like the ant, you had a plan for what to do if you ever lost your job and needed to jump-start your career search. Those new connections would be people you would talk to in hard times, and they would help you seek out new employment prospects. You were prepared for winter, even though you weren't sure when the winds would turn cold and the first snow would fall. But most of us weren't ants. We were grasshoppers. We believed in an endless summer.

We bought houses and cars with monthly payments we couldn't afford. Instead of saving, we bought bigger TVs and the newest model of phone. We believed we would keep getting paid, keep getting bonuses, and keep getting raises at work. In the back of our minds, we knew it couldn't last forever, but we wanted to enjoy it as long as we could.

Summer faded into fall. Banks failed. Houses went into foreclosure. Industries got government bailouts. Stock markets tanked. Grasshoppers lost jobs.

As grasshoppers, we started looking for new

jobs, but we were just one of many grasshoppers in the same situation: unprepared and under-networked. We applied for the same jobs the same way we had in the past: by applying online and emailing our resumes. We hadn't met the influencers in our industry. The ones we did get in touch with were getting contacted by all the other grasshoppers who were out of work.

What About the Ants?

They got laid off too. But the ants had already grown their professional networks. When they saw job openings online, they didn't send their resume to the black hole of the applicant tracking system. They contacted the friends they had made during the summer. More importantly, as they talked with their friends, they found out about jobs that weren't even posted online.

The ants quickly landed new jobs.

The grasshoppers kept looking. Many of them took jobs that were temporary or paid them less than they made before. Some of them never returned to the workforce.

Fast forward to January 1, 2020.

Home prices were hitting fresh, new highs, unemployment was back to 2007 levels, and the stock market was roaring. It was summertime, and the livin' was good.

Once again, everyone talked about how the good times couldn't last. Everyone knew something bad had to happen. An economic winter had to be on the way. The problem was most people weren't doing anything to prepare.

During February 2020, the world started to learn the name of the scourge that would decimate the economy and change the world: COVID-19

In a matter of weeks, the world closed. Driven by government mandates of social distancing, travel stopped, restaurants and stores closed, and tens of millions of people lost their jobs.

Most of us were grasshoppers again.

And the ants were already busy surviving using the networks and connections they created during the good times.

If You Lost Your Job Today, Would You Be Prepared?

When I lost my job the first time, I was a grasshopper. I had worked at the same company for almost a decade, and during that time, I spent no time growing my professional network. It took me three months to find a new job. I told my story earlier, and during my search, I learned the power of professional networking.

As I settled into my new role, I made a

promise to myself: I would never stop networking.

Even if I connected with only one new person each month, I would give time and effort to growing a vibrant professional network. My efforts led to other job opportunities. I switched jobs two more times. Each time, the opportunity came to me through my professional connections.

It was summertime, and if I had remained a grasshopper, I would have sat back and felt great about myself. But I hadn't forgotten the lesson of the first layoff, and I kept working like an ant.

At the end of 2017, I sensed a change coming in the company where I was working. There were problems with the company's financial performance, and job cuts were coming. I didn't know if they would impact me or not, but I started talking to my professional network about opportunities. When I was told my position was being eliminated, I quickly moved to seize the opportunities my network had provided to me.

Being an ant for all those years took my job search from months to weeks. The first time it took me three months. The second time it took me three weeks. The speed at which I found my next job would not have been possible without keeping my network alive.

You've already heard me use the term

"vibrant professional network," but I haven't explained what I mean by the term "vibrant." Vibrant means full of energy and enthusiasm. Does that describe your professional network?

If you contacted the people in your professional network today, would they respond? Would they remember you? Would they think, *I haven't talked to this person in years, and now he's reaching out to me?* This is how people respond to grasshoppers when they connect with their professional network.

Have you ever watched ants work? Do they look like they are full of energy and enthusiasm? Would you think of them as "vibrant"? This type of energy and enthusiasm is what you need when you are growing your vibrant professional network.

What does this look like in practice? It means you interact with your network every day. You make new connections every day. You contact existing connections every day. You add value to your network every day. It sounds time-consuming. This is where people hit an obstacle when it comes to networking because they have a misguided mindset about networking.

Whenever I run into an obstacle that involves a misguided mindset, I have a technique I made up called "language tricks."

Language tricks are ways I change my language to change my mindset. I say the same thing in a slightly different way so that I can change my mind. I use these language tricks to address the two biggest objections I hear when I ask students to complete the following statement at the start of all my coaching sessions: "I know I need to network, but..."

I get many different answers, but the two statements that come out most frequently during this exercise are:

- I'll do it later.
- I don't have time.

Grasshoppers make these statements. Grasshoppers focus on the here and now. Grasshoppers assume there will always be more time. Grasshoppers are the ones who tell me they should have spent more time networking sooner.

To address the first statement, "I'll do it later," I ask the students to change the word "later" to "never." When they make the change it sounds like, "I know I need to network, but I'll do it never."

When you say it like this and say it out loud, it doesn't feel good. I don't want it to feel good. I want it to feel like it's never going to happen if you put it off until later because that's exactly what's going to happen.

The grasshoppers say they'll do it later/never. The ants do it now.

In the second situation, when someone tells

me they "don't have time" to network, I ask them to say the same thing again, but instead of saying, "I don't have time," I tell them to say, "It's not a priority."

When a student of mine says, "I don't network because I don't have time," I ask them to rephrase it and say, "I don't network because it's not a priority." The deeper meaning is if networking is not a priority, then it's not important. Usually, my student responds and says, "Yes, networking is important and is a priority for me, but I don't know how to fit it into my day."

Do you know how many minutes are in each day? 1,440. Everyone gets the same 1,440 minutes each day. We all have the same amount of time each day.

If someone tells me they don't know how to fit networking into their day, I reframe the amount of time each day it takes to grow a vibrant professional network. I tell them all they have to do is spend 1% of their day growing their professional network.

Did you know 1% of your day is 15 minutes? 1% of 1,440 minutes is about 15 minutes.

Investing 1% of your day in an activity that will create opportunities to increase your knowledge or locate talented people for your team or provide you with career insurance seems like a decent return on investment. Spending 1% of your day to shorten a job search from months to weeks seems like a decent way to spend 15 minutes. When I explain it in these terms, the objections about time and priority seem to fade away.

What actions could you take with 1% of your day to help grow your vibrant professional network?

What can you possibly get done today in 15 minutes?

You could:
- Think of one person you know who you have lost touch with over the years.
- Write down that person's name.
- Search for his or her email address or LinkedIn profile.
- Send a quick note that says, "I thought of you today and realized we haven't spoken in a while. How have you been?"

Or you can begin to connect with new people:
- Get on LinkedIn or Twitter or Medium or Quora or Reddit.
- Read an article or post that looks interesting to you.
- Leave an interesting comment. Not a simple, "Nice post," or "Agree," but let the author know what you liked about it and pose a thoughtful, respectful question.
- If the author responds, you can continue

the dialogue.

Or you can find places in the real world to meet new people:
- Search online for an organization that aligns with your interests.
- Find out when their next in-person or online meeting will be.
- Find the name of the organizer.
- Send them an email or message expressing your interest and asking for more information.
- Put the date of the meeting in your calendar.

You could do each of these things in less than 15 minutes. You don't need anyone's permission or approval to start connecting and growing your vibrant professional network.

If you learn one thing from this chapter, it's that you have to start today.

Don't wait for tomorrow.
Don't say, "I don't have time."
Don't say, "I'll do it later."
Don't be a grasshopper.

"Tomorrow is often the busiest day of the week."
—Spanish proverb

CHAPTER 3 – THE LION AND THE MOUSE

Once when a Lion was asleep, a little Mouse began running up and down upon him; this soon awakened the Lion, who placed his huge paw upon him, and opened his big jaws to swallow him.

"Pardon, O King," cried the little Mouse: "forgive me this time, I shall never forget it: who knows but what I may be able to do you a turn some of these days?"

The Lion was so tickled at the idea of the Mouse being able to help him, that he lifted up his paw and let him go. Sometime after the Lion was caught in a trap, and the hunters who desired to carry him alive to the King, tied him to a tree while they went in search of a wagon to carry him on.

Just then the little Mouse happened to pass

by, and seeing the sad plight in which the Lion was, went up to him and soon gnawed away the ropes that bound the King of the Beasts. "Was I not right?" said the little Mouse:

Little friends may prove great friends.

When we think of growing our vibrant professional networks, we believe we need to connect with important people: CEOs, CFOs, COOs, CHROs, or anyone with a "Chief" in his or her job title.

We want to connect with people we think are powerful because we believe they know a lot of important people and can introduce us to them. We believe people of influence are the only ones who can help us, but the fable teaches us something different.

Focusing on influencers is hard. They get lots of requests from lots of people. If you don't know them or have a relationship with them, they may not give you an opportunity to talk to them. Not because they aren't good people, but because they get a lot of requests. If they start responding to all of them, they will never get anything else done.

As you grow your professional network, be different from all the people who are vying for the attention of people in high places: start with people you already know.

You Never Know Who Might Be Able to Help You

When I give this advice, I hear people say, "I don't know anyone." What they really mean is they don't know anyone they think is important enough to connect with.

Everyone knows someone. You know your family. You know your friends. You know your classmates. If you've had one job, you know your co-workers. If you've had multiple jobs, you know many more people.

In his book *Give and Take*,[3] Adam Grant explains a concept called "dormant ties." Dormant ties are people you've worked with in the past but have lost touch with. This concept is based on a study by the MIT Sloan School of Management where a group of executives was asked to make a list of people they had worked with in the past but had lost contact with over the years.[4]

The executives were asked to send an email to these former colleagues and ask for their opinions on problems the executives were facing in their organizations. The executives

---

[3] Adam Grant, *Give and Take: Why Helping Others Drives Our Success* (New York: Penguin Random House, LLC, 2014)
[4] Daniel Z. Levin, Jorge Walter, J. Keith Murnighan, "The Power of Reconnection - How Dormant Ties Can Surprise You," MIT Sloan Management Review 52, no. 3 (March 2011): 45-40.

believed some of their dormant ties would respond, but they were surprised to find the response rate was higher than they expected.

The advice they received was also much more innovative and diverse than advice they received from people they interacted with every day.

The conclusion was the dormant ties already knew and trusted the executives from their past work experience, and due to these professional relationships, they were willing to help them. Also, because these dormant ties had moved on to other endeavors, they had a different set of experiences to draw on when giving the executives advice. This led to new perspectives that helped the executives think creatively about the problems they were solving.

We All Have Dormant Ties

Even if you are not an executive who is solving your organization's problems, there are people you have worked with in the past who you have lost touch with. Reconnecting with them will jump-start your professional network for a few reasons:

- **You have a place to start.** You can create a list of people you already know. You don't need to do a ton of research on these people. Simply think about all the

people you've worked with in the past and write their names down on a list.
- **You have their contact info.** There's a good chance you either have email addresses for your dormant ties or you know how to find them. Again, this removes the barrier of searching for information on these people. If you don't have their contact info, you may already be connected with them through LinkedIn or other social media.
- **These people recognize your name.** When you contact them, they're going to see your name and respond to your message. Your message isn't going to go into the trash folder with all the other unsolicited emails they receive.

These three reasons form the basis of trust with your dormant ties. If you have worked with someone, you most likely already trust them, and they trust you. Of course, there are people you have worked with you never want to interact with again, but these are probably exceptions and not the rule.

It should go without saying, but I am going to say it anyway: If there was someone you didn't get along with at a previous employer, don't waste your time trying to connect with them. It's not a good use of your time.

For the rest of your dormant ties where there

is a level of trust when you reconnect with them, they're going to recognize your name, read your message, and respond.

People I coach on professional networking, in particular introverts, usually have the following objections when I ask them why they don't network:

- I don't know anyone.
- I don't know where to start.
- I don't want to cold call or cold email anyone.
- I don't know what to say to people I am contacting.

Starting with dormant ties eliminates these objections.

However, some people who are starting to grow their vibrant professional networks don't believe this dormant-tie approach will work. That's okay. The executives in the MIT study didn't think it would work either.

I commonly hear my students say things like, "Reconnecting with people I already know doesn't seem like networking. These people are already in my network. I'm trying to meet new people."

I understand this perspective. At the same time, remember, we are growing a vibrant professional network to create mutually beneficial opportunities for ourselves and for the people in our network. Also, remember, "vibrant" means "active and alive." When we reconnect with our "dormant" ties, we activate them and make them vibrant again. If we find opportunities through people we already know, what's the difference between dormant ties who become vibrant and new people we add to our network?

For students who are convinced they need to meet new people, I ask them, "How did you meet most of the people you know today?" It's usually through proximity. In other words, people who are close to them in their lives. We know the people who are in our neighborhood, in our school, in our workplace, or in our community groups.

The other way we meet people is through introductions from other people. We very rarely meet new connections who started as random people on the street that we walked up and started talking to.

Our dormant ties are the people who we know through proximity, and over time, when you connect with them, the opportunity will arise for them to introduce you to someone new. The person who introduces you makes the link, and because he or she knows you and the new person you are meeting, there is a level of trust between yourself and this new person based on your common acquaintance's endorsement of you and your new friend.

For people who still don't believe in the dormant-tie approach, I share this story with them:

I got a thank you note from one of my group coaching participants.

It started like this:

"I wanted to extend a huge thank you for your expertise, time, and commitment to organizing these virtual events. I'm writing you this note, right after signing the job offer letter, and all of this was possible by listening to your advice and executing the steps discussed in our calls."

It was from a student of mine named Mary. She had relocated and had no network in a new city. Besides not knowing anyone, she was worried about her job because changes were happening in her company. She saw a post about my group coaching program to help people grow their professional networks. She gave it a try. It led her to a brand-new job.

What sort of networking magic did I teach her that led to a job offer? No magic. Just the power of dormant ties. Dormant ties are a goldmine in your professional network.

In my group coaching program, I ask everyone to make a list of five people they already know and get in touch with them. That's how Mary's journey from "no network in a new city" to "a brand-new job" started. She got in touch with a manager she used to work with, and he asked her if she was interested in an open position at his company.

Her letter to me continued:

"He was one of the five initial contacts I sent emails to, as you advised. I hadn't spoken to him for over a year...The entire job searching process took me exactly one month from the initial conversation about the opportunity to the offer letter. I am shocked, to say the least, *as one simple note could lead to a life-changing event.*"

One simple note to a person she had worked with in the past was all it took to create this opportunity.

Your dormant ties are the mouse in the fable. Most of them aren't going to be powerful lions who lead companies. They are going to be people just like you. But they can make a difference. They can help you find opportunities. They can help you meet new people. All you need to do is reconnect with them.

In the *Ant and the Grasshopper* chapter, I told you to write down one person's name who you had lost touch with and to connect with them. If you haven't already done that, do it now.

But don't stop there.

- Look at your resume or LinkedIn profile and start with the last job you had.
- Think of the people you worked with at

that job.
- Write down the names of everyone you can remember. If you need help remembering who worked there, visualize what the office looked like and take a mental walk around the office. Who are the people you see? Add their names to the list.

Another way to find dormant ties is to look at the name of the companies you worked for on LinkedIn.

- In LinkedIn, you can find the names of all the people who have the company listed on their profile. Scroll through this list.
- Who are you already a 1st-degree connection with but haven't talked to in a long time? Add these people to your list if they aren't already on it.
- Who are the people who are 2nd-degree connections that you know well enough to send a connection request to? Add these people to the list of people you are going to connect with.
- Do this for every company where you have worked.

At the end of this exercise, you will have a list of people to connect with. It may be five people long or it may be five hundred people long. The number is not important. In fact, right now, I would encourage you to focus on the first five names on the list. Send them an email or a LinkedIn message saying, "I thought of you today and realized we haven't spoken in a while. How have you been?"

That's all it takes to reconnect with your dormant ties and begin the process of converting them from dormant to vibrant members of your professional network.

It's a simple note. Don't overthink it. You already know most of the people who will create your vibrant professional network. As in the fable, no one is too small or unimportant to be in your network, and as you saw from Mary's story, you are only one connection away from a life-changing opportunity.

> *"Lots of people want to ride with you in the limo, but what you want is someone who will take the bus with you when the limo breaks down."*
> *—Oprah Winfrey*

CHAPTER 4 – THE CROW AND THE PITCHER

A Crow, half-dead with thirst, came upon a Pitcher which had once been full of water; but when the Crow put its beak into the mouth of the Pitcher he found that only very little water was left in it and that he could not reach far enough down to get at it.

He tried, and he tried, but at last, he had to give up in despair. Then a thought came to him, and he took a pebble and dropped it into the Pitcher. Then he took another pebble and dropped it into the Pitcher. Then he took another pebble and dropped that into the Pitcher. Then he took another pebble and dropped that into the Pitcher. Then he took another pebble and dropped that into the Pitcher. Then he took another pebble and dropped that into the Pitcher.

At last, at last, he saw the water mount up near him, and after casting in a few more pebbles he was able to quench his thirst and save his life.

Little by little does the trick.

Mark was getting frustrated. He'd been working with our coaching group for a couple of weeks and didn't feel like he'd made any progress. He'd made a list of his dormant ties who were mostly former classmates and people he had worked with. He'd started sending emails and LinkedIn messages following my advice to connect online, followed by setting up phone calls or in-person meetings.

For all his work, he felt like he wasn't getting any responses. He felt like his efforts were being wasted. Then one week, everything changed.

During one of our calls, he shared a revelation that helped him get past his frustration and continue to make connections.

He told us, "Whenever I hesitate to send an email or a message to someone I want to connect with, I ask myself, 'What's the marginal cost of sending this?'"

His point was the cost to send an email message was low. If the person ignored him, nothing was lost, but if a person connected with him, there could be a huge payoff.

During the time he was in the group, Mark

was looking for a job and had found some opportunities to start his own consulting business. He realized that instead of using networking to find a job, he was going to need to use it to find new clients.

Sending the first note to someone you want to connect with seems like such a small thing. It doesn't seem like it could possibly make a difference. The impact of the effort seems so low, but the accumulation of the notes and messages, which cost you little to send, can turn into a huge opportunity.

I tell my students once they have their list of dormant ties, the next step is to send them a simple message via email or LinkedIn: "I thought of you today and realized we haven't spoken in a while. How have you been?"

Sometimes, your dormant ties won't respond to your message for weeks or even months. Don't get discouraged. People are busy. They have a lot of things going on. Ask yourself, "Have I ever let an email sit in my inbox for a while before responding?" But in most cases, you will get a response. What then?

Your goal is to take the online email or LinkedIn message and turn it into a face-to-face or voice-to-voice conversation. Remember, you're trying to grow a deep professional relationship. To do this, you need to actually talk to the other person. Having this conversation is the first step. If a face-to-face conversation isn't possible due to geography, schedules, or social distancing, then have a voice-to-voice conversation on a phone or video call.

People try to overthink this step. They think this needs to be a formal conversation or have some type of agenda. I remind them they're talking to someone they already know. They don't need to impress this person, and they definitely don't need to give this person some sort of elevator pitch. Instead, they need to have a conversation with a former colleague to catch up on what's going on in their lives.

Even with this guidance, my students commonly ask me, "What are we going to talk about?" My answer is "If you don't know what to talk about, you can ask your connections about their favorite topic."

Everyone in the world has the same favorite topic.

It's the topic they know the most about: **THEMSELVES.**

Your job in this conversation is easy: Ask the person about themselves, and then listen to what they say. Don't interrupt or zone out or look at your phone. Really listen to what they say.

- What have they been working on?
- What have they been struggling with?
- What or who do they wish they already knew?

The answers to these questions are going to be the key to developing your deep professional relationship and growing your vibrant professional network. When you have one of these conversations, you're going to walk away feeling great and looking forward to all the opportunities that could come out of this connection.

You'll go your separate ways, promising to stay in touch and assuring yourselves you will look for ways to help one another.

A few days go by. You don't hear back from your new connection. The one pebble you worked so hard to drop in your professional networking pitcher didn't really make a difference.

What now?

You stay focused on your goal of creating a vibrant professional network and keep sending emails to your other dormant ties. You make another connection. Another conversation takes place. You feel good about the discussion and look forward to developing a professional relationship with your connections.

A few days go by. That second pebble didn't make a difference either.

This is when the frustration sets in. This is when people start thinking they are bad at networking. This is when people give up and stop trying to connect with people. They don't keep dropping pebbles because they don't see any progress.

In our fable, if the crow had stopped dropping pebble after pebble into the pitcher, he would have died of thirst.

In professional networking, if you stop making connections on a regular basis, your network will cease to exist.

It's tempting to give up after a few connections fail to deliver a new job opportunity or an introduction to someone you really want to meet. But if you stop after a few connections, not only have you halted any progress to grow your professional network, but you have also squandered the effort you put into the first few connections you made.

Each of these connections is part of growing your professional network. The second one builds on the first. The third builds on the second. Connection after connection builds until your professional networking pitcher is overflowing with opportunities.

In *Atomic Habits*,[5] James Clear tells a story about the boiling point of water to demonstrate that all our efforts accumulate on themselves. If you add one degree of temperature to a pot of water at 200 degrees Fahrenheit, it's not going to boil. If you add another degree, it's also not

---

[5] James Clear, *Atomic Habits: An Easy & Proven Way to Build Good Habits & Break Bad Ones* (New York: Penguin Random House, LLC, 2018)

going to boil. You add degree after degree of temperature (energy) until you get to 211 degrees; however, at this point, the water is still not boiling. But if you add one more degree and the temperature reaches 212 degrees, the water boils. There is nothing special about that last degree of energy. It was all the other energy, added together, cumulatively, that raised the temperature to a boiling point.

For your network to grow, you need to add the first connection. While this connection may not be the source of some life-changing opportunity, you must start with your first connection. Without the first connection, you don't get a second connection. Without the second connection, you don't make a third connection. As you continue to connect, many of your existing connections will intersect and people you never expected will know each other.

A word of caution: sometimes people focus on putting the pebbles into the pitcher all at once. They try to do a weekend sprint where they send out a whole slew of emails or LinkedIn messages to their dormant ties. They try to have multiple networking conversations in one day. While this may be a necessity if you are looking for a job, it's not sustainable and not recommended. People who try to do this end up getting overwhelmed and frustrated and stop dropping any pebbles into their networking pitcher.

At some point, your networking pitcher will be too full of pebbles and you can't fit any more in. This is a good problem to have and one which you can control by focusing on quality over quantity in your professional relationships. We'll talk more about this in the chapter *The Hare Who Had Many Friends*.

The pebbles are the small actions you take to grow your vibrant professional network.

The pitcher is our professional network.

The water is the opportunity our network brings us.

We think that one connection won't do the job. And we are right. One connection isn't going to get us to the water.

We need the cumulative power of all the connections we make.

What pebbles can you drop into your pitcher today?

- Pick a name from your list of dormant ties and send an initial email. Remember, keep it simple.
- If a dormant tie has already responded, set up that face-to-face or voice-to-voice conversation.
- When you have the conversation, really listen to what the person has to say.
- Make a mental note of ways you could help them based on the conversation.

Do this once a day. Every day.

As Mark told our coaching group, the cost of doing these small things is low. There's no reason you shouldn't be dropping a lot of these pebbles into the pitcher.

"It is a mistake to look too far ahead. Only one link of the chain of destiny can be handled at a time."
— Winston Churchill

CHAPTER 5 – THE MISER AND HIS GOLD

Once upon a time, there was a Miser who used to hide his gold at the foot of a tree in his garden; but every week he used to go and dig it up and gloat over his gains. A robber, who had noticed this, went and dug up the gold and decamped with it. When the Miser next came to gloat over his treasures, he found nothing but the empty hole. He tore his hair and raised such an outcry that all the neighbors came around him, and he told them how he used to come and visit his gold. "Did you ever take any of it out?" asked one of them.

"Nay," said he, "I only came to look at it."

"Then come again and look at the hole," said a neighbor; "it will do you just as much good."

Wealth unused might as well not exist.

When I work with people to help them grow their networks, I often hear them tell me they don't like to network because they hate asking for help from other people. They feel like they're taking advantage of other people or inconveniencing them.

In many cases, when people are networking, they're asking someone to help them find a new job. They envision themselves asking people in their network to give their resume to someone or to introduce them to the person who is making the final hiring decision.

They're hesitant to ask for help because they put themselves in the other person's shoes and know if someone was asking for their help, they would feel uncomfortable, even burdened by the ask.

When someone asks us to do something for them, it can often feel like we're doing all the work for them. We resent being asked to do one more thing. We feel taken advantage of. We find excuses not to help them.

When we need help, we remember that feeling, and we don't want to saddle people with our problems.

There is a way to approach networking that will help alleviate the feeling of taking advantage of people.

When someone asks you for help, who are you more likely to help? Someone who has helped you in the past or someone who hasn't?

If someone has helped you or given you something of value, aren't you more likely to help that person? Don't you feel a certain sense of reciprocity toward them? Don't you want to return the favor to them?

The Principle of Reciprocity is the first of six principles discussed in Robert Cialdini's book, *Influence: The Psychology of Persuasion*.[6] Cialdini summarizes this principle by saying: "Simply put, people are obliged to give back to others the form of a behavior, gift, or service that they have received first."

He then goes on to explain experiments in restaurants where some customers were given a small gift—a fortune cookie or a mint—with their bill. Those who were given the gift gave higher tips than those who were not given the gift. My wife, a singer and actress who used to supplement her income waiting tables confirmed this finding with her personal experience. In some restaurants she worked in, the owners gave away desserts and other gifts to customers while other owners had strict rules against giving anything away.

The restaurants that gave food away made

---

[6] Robert Cialdini, *Principles of Persuasion: Influence at Work, Reciprocity*, https://www.influenceatwork.com/principles-of-persuasion/#reciprocity

the customers feel special and inspired them to not only spend more but to keep coming back and to tell their friends about how great the restaurant was.

The restaurants that didn't give anything away were places where customers came in one time and never came back again.

Cialdini explains, "The key to using the Principle of Reciprocity is to be the first to give and to ensure that what you give is personalized and unexpected."

If you lead with giving, people will want to reciprocate and give back to you. You don't even have to ask for help. People will ask you what they can do to help you.

The next question that comes up is: "What do I have to give?"

You have much more to give than you know. You're unique. You have a unique set of knowledge and perspectives.

To you, what you know is ordinary because you spend all day knowing the things you know. You are like the miser and his gold. The ideas in your head are your gold, and if you dig them up and look at them without ever sharing any of them, they do you as much good as if you never had them at all. As in the fable, you need to share what you know with the world for it to have any value.

The ideas you have are what you can give when you're in a conversation with one of your professional connections. When you sit down in a face-to-face or voice-to-voice conversation with a dormant tie or a new connection, you're already listening to what is going on with them because you have asked them to tell you about themselves. Think about what you can give to them:

- Advice
- Recommendations
- Introductions

Remember, from *The Bundle of Sticks* fable, one of the reasons to network is knowledge and authority. Sharing your knowledge and authority can help your connection solve whatever problem he is working on.

You may have an idea your connection has never heard.

It's hard to believe that everyone doesn't know all the same things you know. It's called the "curse for knowledge." Once we learn something, we lose the perspective of being a beginner and the feeling of what it was like to not have that knowledge. Because we lose that perspective, we can't imagine what it's like to not know what we've learned and assume everyone else knows the same thing.

A 2006 *Harvard Business Review* article explained the curse of knowledge by describing an experiment using well-known songs:[7]

"In 1990, a Stanford University graduate student in psychology named Elizabeth Newton illustrated the curse of knowledge by studying a simple game in which she assigned people to one of two roles: "tapper" or "listener." Each tapper was asked to pick a well-known song, such as "Happy Birthday," and tap out the rhythm on a table. The listener's job was to guess the song.

Over the course of Newton's experiment, 120 songs were tapped out. Listeners guessed only three of the songs correctly: a success ratio of 2.5%. But before they guessed, Newton asked the tappers to predict the probability that listeners would guess correctly. They predicted 50%. The tappers got their message across one time in 40, but they thought they would get it across one time in two. Why?

When a tapper taps, it is impossible for her to avoid hearing the tune playing along to her taps. Meanwhile, all the listener can hear is a kind of bizarre Morse code. Yet the tappers were flabbergasted by how hard the listeners had to work to pick up the tune.

The problem is that once we know something — say, the melody of a song — we find

---

[7] Chip Heath, Dan Heath, "The Curse of Knowledge," *Harvard Business Review* 84, no. 12 (December 2006):
https://hbr.org/2006/12/the-curse-of-knowledge

it hard to imagine not knowing it. Our knowledge has "cursed" us. We have difficulty sharing it with others because we can't readily re-create their state of mind."

Share the knowledge you have even if you think everyone already knows it. You'll be surprised how often you give your connection something of value when you share the nuggets of your personal wisdom.

Besides sharing knowledge and authority, we can provide recommendations. These might be books or articles your connection can read or videos and speeches she should watch. This is like knowledge and authority, but recommendations are more tangible because you can share a link or a specific source outside your own knowledge.

In some cases, your recommendation may be another person your connection should meet. In this situation, you can introduce your connection to the other person you know. This allows your connection to grow his network.

For introductions, I advise people to handle them carefully. If you are going to introduce your connection to someone you already know, you need to be sure that the person you already know is open to connecting with new people. The best way to find this out is to ask the person you already know if she would be open to meeting your connection.

Let's look at this using Susie and Bob. Susie

is the person you would like your professional connection, Bob, to meet. As you are talking to Bob, you think of Susie as someone to introduce him to. You tell Bob about Susie but say, "I like to respect the time of my professional connections, so I am going to ask Susie if she would be open to an introduction. If she is, I will connect the two of you."

When you connect with Susie, you describe Bob and explain why you think it would be mutually beneficial for her to talk to him. Ask permission to connect the two of them via an email. If she doesn't answer or says no, respect that decision. Go back to Bob and explain the situation and then try to provide another idea, recommendation, or introduction.

If she says yes, send a simple email that says, "Susie, per our earlier conversation, I wanted to introduce you to Bob. Bob is a connection of mine looking to grow his network, and I thought you would be a great person to connect with. Bob, Susie is a person you should connect with. I'll let you two take the conversation from here."

You could add more context to the email about Susie or Bob's background and why they would be valuable connections, but it doesn't have to be verbose. Don't overdo it.

What if you are having a conversation with one of your networking connections and you can't think of anything to give? If all else fails, you can give them something everyone has: your attention.

When you are sitting in a conversation with another person and you feel like you have her complete and total attention, you feel good. You feel heard. You feel connected to the other person. You like them. You want to build a relationship with her.

That's how other people feel when you give them your attention. They want to create a deeper professional relationship with you. They want to find ways to help you, and when that happens, you remove the awkwardness most people feel when they are networking and asking people to help them. Having a giving mindset in professional networking and trying to help other people first makes everything about networking easier and more comfortable.

But most people think about networking the way the miser felt about his gold: they want to keep all of their resources, all of their knowledge, and all of their attention buried in a hole. They want to hold on to it and not share it with anyone else because they are worried that if they give their ideas and their knowledge away, other people will take them and use them for their own purposes. They are afraid they won't get the credit or benefit of their thoughts.

If you don't give away what you have to offer, your gifts do you as much good as the gold in the hole. As in the story, they are as valuable as not having them at all.

You need to give what you have to other people, especially to people you're creating a relationship with. The best part about what you can give is it's better than the gold in the fable. That is, a gold coin can only be given away one time, but your knowledge and attention can be given away over and over to multiple people. They can be spent multiple times. However, if you don't give them away, their value will never come back to you.

When it comes to professional networking, don't be a miser.

> *"For it is in giving that we receive."*
> *—Saint Francis of Assisi*

CHAPTER 6 – THE HARE WHO HAD MANY FRIENDS

A Hare was very popular with the other beasts who all claimed to be her friends. But one day she heard the hounds approaching and hoped to escape them by the aid of her many Friends. So, she went to the horse, and asked him to carry her away from the hounds on his back. But he declined, stating that he had important work to do for his master. "He felt sure," he said, "that all her other friends would come to her assistance." She then applied to the bull and hoped that he would repel the hounds with his horns. The bull replied: "I am very sorry, but I have an appointment with a lady; but I feel sure that our friend the goat will do what you want." The ram replied: "Another time, my dear friend. I do not like to interfere on the present occasion, as hounds have been known to eat sheep as well as hares." The Hare then applied, as a last hope, to the calf, who regretted that he was unable to help her, as he did not like to take the responsibility upon himself, as so many older persons than himself had declined the task. By this time, the hounds were quite near, and the Hare took to her heels and luckily escaped.

She that has many friends, has no friends.

The fable of *The Hare Who Had Many Friends* illustrates two concepts critical to growing a vibrant professional network. The first concept is creating relationships. In the fable, the hare seems to have a lot of friends, but she doesn't have many relationships. She has quantity, but not quality. Her "friends" don't come to her rescue.

Do you know a hare? Someone who seems to know everyone? When we talk to a hare, she tells us about the people she knows.

There are people on LinkedIn who try to amass the largest number of connections and followers they can. They brag about how many connections they have. If you're connected to these people, there's little chance these people know who you are. Their goal is not to develop deep professional relationships; instead, they're trying to create a following, an audience.

There is nothing wrong with growing an

audience, but if you're trying to grow a vibrant professional network, these people are not the ones you should be imitating on LinkedIn. These people are like the hares. They appear popular online, but it's unlikely their followers would come to their aid if they were in need.

A hare is sometimes called something else: a name-dropper. Most people don't like the name-dropper. The size of his network sounds impressive, but we wonder, does he really know all these important people? If we talked to the people whose names he drops, would they know our name-dropper?

Even if these people do know who our name-dropper is, do they have enough of a relationship with him to help him when he needs it? In our fable, the hare knows everyone, but none of them felt inclined to help her when she needed it.

Think about yourself for a minute. When a person asks you for help, are you more likely to help if you just met her or if you have a professional relationship with her?

It's an easy answer.

You're going to help people who you have built a relationship with. You're going to help someone who has given something to you in the past. As we discussed in the chapter about the miser and his gold, when people give something to us, we want to reciprocate.

Every day, I get connection requests from

people on LinkedIn. Most of these are from people I have never met before. They found me on LinkedIn and decided to send me a connection request. Unless the profile looks fake, I accept the connection request. Sometimes, right after I accept the request, I receive a message asking me to consider buying whatever the person is selling. Most of these are automated messages, impersonal and not aligned with my interests. I rarely respond to these.

In other cases, I receive a new connection request from someone, and they spend time developing a relationship with me before they ask for my help.

That's what Larry did.

Larry had recently lost his job and was trying to connect with people who could help him get an interview. Instead of sending me a connection request and immediately asking me for help, he connected with me through one of my existing connections, Debbie.

Debbie knew Larry and sent me a message through LinkedIn saying I should meet him. Right away, this made Larry a more interesting connection for me. He was being introduced by someone I already knew and trusted. Because Debbie was someone in my network with whom I had a professional relationship, I wanted to help her by helping her friend Larry.

Even though we were connected through a

mutual friend, Larry still took the time to go farther than simply asking me for help. He asked if we could have a short phone call to get to know each other better. He tried to grow a relationship through a voice-to-voice conversation.

When we talked, I could tell Larry would be someone I would recommend for a job. His background and experience were impressive, and he was articulate. I knew if a hiring manager talked to him, she would be impressed by him.

I doubt I would have felt the same way if I had simply received an email or LinkedIn request from him. The extra effort to grow the relationship made me more willing to help him.

After our conversation, Larry did something else that illustrates the second concept from the fable of the hare:

He made it easy for me to help him.

In the fable, the hare has a big ask of her friends: save her from the hounds. For most of the animals, this meant putting themselves in danger to save the hare. In fact, the ram says, "hounds have been known to eat sheep as well as hares." He doesn't want to put himself in jeopardy to help the hare.

The horse and the bull didn't want to get involved and made excuses not to help.

Everyone had different reasons not to help. Perhaps if she had asked for one of the animals to simply provide a distraction for the hounds so she had time to get away, the animals may have been more willing to help.

If you're hard to help, people will find reasons not to help you. Everyone has a lot going on. If what you ask people to do takes too much time or energy, they won't get around to it. Not because they don't want to but because they have other priorities.

What does it look like when you're hard to help?

Let's think about applying for a job.

If you ask a professional connection to take your resume and give it to someone in recruiting, that's being hard to help. Your connection must take your resume, find the recruiter, then hand it to them and tell them to call you. The recruiter must believe you are someone they should call, and then call you.

There are too many places this could go wrong.

Your connection may print out your resume and leave it on the side of his desk while figuring out who to give it to. He gets busy and your resume gets buried on his desk. Or he gives it to the recruiter, and he thinks, *That's it. I've done my job helping my connection*, but the recruiter doesn't call you because she is busy, and your resume gets buried in the pile on her desk.

You never get anywhere in the interviewing process because you were too hard to help. Instead of asking your connection to "pass my resume to the right person," ask him to introduce you to the right person, which is the person making the hiring decision for the job. This is easier for your connection to do. He can introduce you by email and you can do the rest. Making the task easier means you'll have a better chance of being helped.

What are other ways to be easy to help?

The best way is to be specific about what you want your connection to do.

- Who is the person you want to meet?
- What companies are ones where you want to meet someone?
- What industry do you want to learn more about?

The more specific and the simpler the ask, the more likely you are to get help.

When I talk to people about networking to find a job, I tell them to create a target list of companies. This is what Larry did to make himself easy to help. After our conversation on the phone, he sent me an email with a list of companies where he was interested in working.

It was an actual document, well-crafted and well-formatted.

This is exactly what I tell the students in my group to do when we are talking about being easy to help. I tell them the target list needs to be a physical list that can be handed to connections or emailed to them. The reason it needs to be a physical list is twofold.

First, when you have a list of companies where you want to meet people who can help you get a job, you prime your connection's brain and make it easier for her to think of people. The list of companies will cue your connection to flip through her mental Rolodex and think of people with whom she can connect you. You are creating an availability bias in your connection's brain.

Availability bias "is a mental shortcut that relies on immediate examples that come to a given person's mind when evaluating a specific topic, concept, method or decision."[8] Your target list of companies gives your connection a set of available information, the list of companies, to make it easier for her brain to think about who she knows at those companies. Your target list narrows down the list of possible people your connection knows so that she can focus on a smaller list of all the people

---

[8] Wikipedia, *Availability heuristic*,
https://en.wikipedia.org/wiki/Availability_heuristic

she can introduce you to. Even if she doesn't know someone at the companies on your list, it helps her think of other companies to add to your list.

The second reason your list needs to be a physical list is if the person can take the list with her, she is more likely to remember you and remember what you are looking for. A funny thing will happen when your connection takes the list with her: subconsciously she will start seeing the companies on your list in her everyday life.

Your list has primed her brain to continue using part of the availability bias, which makes our brains use the most recent information it has received. Your connection will start noticing the names of the companies on your list online in news articles, in advertisements, or online job postings.

Of course, she would have seen the names of these companies whether she met you or not, but without your target list, she would have simply ignored the names of these companies when she saw them. Her brain wouldn't have been primed to notice them.

Instead, the names of the companies on your list are fresh in her brain, or she will continue to look at the names on your list because she took it with her. When she sees the names of the companies in her daily life, your name will come to her mind; she will let you know about the opportunities she sees, and put you in touch with the people you need to talk to. Putting your list into the subconsciousness of more people means you have "opportunity scouts" out in the world unknowingly searching for opportunities for you.

Also, it's easier for her to take your target company list with her than it is to take your resume. Taking your resume implies she has a commitment to give it to someone else. She feels more pressure to do something with your resume. It makes it harder for her to help you if she takes your resume.

Taking your target company list means all she must do is let you know if she sees any opportunities at the companies on your target list. It's much easier for her to look for opportunities than to send your resume to someone else, which means you are making it easier for her to help you.

Larry provided me with his target company list. He also gave me specific types of jobs he was qualified for and interested in. I happened to know that there were some jobs of that type open at the company I was working for at the time. Because we had developed a professional relationship through our conversation and because he had made it easy to help him, I was able to send an email to the person who was hiring for these jobs. All I did was ask the hiring manager if he was still looking for people for the role. It was one simple email and easy for me. The hiring manager said yes, and I sent Larry's information to him.

Several weeks after I sent Larry's information to the hiring manager, I got an email from Larry. It came to my internal business email. Larry was emailing me from our company email system. He had gotten the job!

We had another phone conversation, and he explained that after I sent the information to the hiring manager, he called Larry. They had an initial phone interview. Then more interviews. It all moved forward after I provided the initial introduction.

As I said, Larry was an impressive candidate, and I wasn't surprised he had gotten the job, but he let me know that he didn't think he would have had the chance to show what he could do if I hadn't sent his information to the hiring manager.

Unlike the hare in the fable, Larry developed a real relationship. He didn't focus on meeting hundreds of people online and asking them for help. He focused on getting to know people who could help him, and most importantly, he made himself easy to help.

> *"We can't help everyone, but everyone can help someone."*
> *—Ronald Reagan*

CHAPTER 7 — THE HARE AND THE TORTOISE

The Hare was once boasting of his speed before the other animals. "I have never yet been beaten," said he, "when I put forth my full speed. I challenge any one here to race with me."

The Tortoise said quietly, "I accept your challenge."

"That is a good joke," said the Hare; "I could dance round you all the way."

"Keep your boasting till you've beaten me," answered the Tortoise. "Shall we race?"

So a course was fixed and a start was made. The Hare darted almost out of sight at once, but soon stopped and, to show his contempt for the Tortoise, lay down to have a nap. The Tortoise plodded on and plodded on, and when the Hare awoke from his nap, he saw the Tortoise just near the winning-post and could not run up in time to save the race. Then said the Tortoise:

Plodding wins the race.

I'm sure you've been waiting for this one. This might be the most well-known of Aesop's fables. Everyone has heard the fable of The Hare and The Tortoise. We know the lessons:

- Don't go fast.
- Don't stop.
- Those who start fast won't last.

Yet, we need to be reminded over and over that slow and steady wins the race. I usually teach people about professional networking through articles, webinars, or in-person and online coaching. When I get to the end of the lessons, I use this fable to highlight that growing your professional network isn't a project you can finish in one weekend. It's a journey that takes time and requires you to keep going.

In the previous fables, I've described actions anyone can take to grow a vibrant professional network:

- Start with who you know by reconnecting with dormant ties.
- Connect online but create professional relationships through in-person or voice-to-voice conversations.

- Give before you get.
- Be easy to help by being specific about who you want to meet.

These actions create a cycle. When you go through the cycle, you'll come to the end of it and get introduced to someone new. Your network grows and you repeat the cycle. But if you only do this cycle once, your network will stop growing.

You must keep going.

You must take these actions every day.

Readers with a keen eye might ask, "How is the lesson from *The Hare and the Tortoise* fable different from *The Crow and the Pitcher* story?"

Remember, the crow had to drop pebble after pebble into the pitcher to drink the water. When you're growing your professional network, you need to take many small steps, like the pebbles, in order to reach your goal. But once you've reached a goal of connecting with a new person, you need to keep going, like the tortoise in this fable. You can't stop dropping pebbles in the pitcher and take a nap like the hare. You can't expect one sprint of connecting with a few people is going to give you a vibrant professional network.

Most people think about professional networking as something to do when you're looking for a new job. It feels like work to network. It feels like a project to get done. It feels like something with a definite start and stop time.

However, the people with the strongest, most vibrant networks are the ones who connect with their network every day.

At the same time, they don't spend all day, every day, networking. Instead, they make their networking actions small and sustainable. They create a networking habit.

Habits are strange things. Bad habits are so easy to create. Good habits feel difficult to form.

Recently, there has been a lot of research around how humans form habits. A Stanford professor and researcher named BJ Fogg has created an approach called Tiny Habits to help people create new habits in their lives. He highlights his approach in his book called *Tiny Habits: The Small Changes that Change Everything*.[9]

The key concept of the Tiny Habits approach is to make the action you want to turn into a habit tinier. Tiny actions help overcome any lack of motivation you have for doing the action. The example Fogg frequently gives is the habit of flossing your teeth. He explains that when you want to create this habit, instead of saying you're going to floss your teeth, you tell yourself you're going to floss one tooth. That's

---

[9] BJ Fogg, *Tiny Habits: The Small Changes That Change Everything* (Boston: Houghton Mifflin Harcourt, 2020)

it, just one tooth. The point is most people believe they can floss one tooth. The act is so tiny, it's almost impossible not to do it. Once you've flossed one tooth, you realize you can floss more teeth, and you'll floss all of your teeth.

Why does the Tiny Habits approach work? Most of us face resistance when we think of starting something new. We think about the work it's going to be. We think of the steps we need to take. We think of how much time we're going to have to commit to form a new habit or complete a new project. We get overwhelmed, so we never get started.

In the Tiny Habits method, the things we need to do are made smaller. Whatever tasks are part of the new habit we want to create are reduced to a ridiculously tiny action to overcome any resistance. The reduction in the size of the task gets us past our mental resistance. After we've had success with the tiny action, we feel a sense of accomplishment, and we believe we can keep going. As we keep going, we form the habit. In time, we can't imagine a time when we didn't do the thing that has become a habit.

How does the Tiny Habits approach apply to professional networking?

To apply the Tiny Habits method, you need to think about how you can make all of the actions we have talked about tinier:

- Instead of deciding to contact ten dormant ties, reconnect with one.
- Instead of sending emails or LinkedIn messages to ten people, send one.
- Instead of having five in-person or voice-to-voice conversations this week, have one.
- Instead of trying to think of seven ways to help someone else, think of one.

As you grow your professional network, when you feel overwhelmed and can't get started or keep going, think to yourself, *How can I make this action tinier?*

Let's say you're extremely motivated to grow your professional network. You decide this weekend, you're going to sit down and find 100 dormant ties and send them emails to set up time to talk to them next week. Like the hare, do you think that might wear you out and require that you take a break and rest? Do you think it might be tough to do that every weekend? Do you think that if you did that once, you could keep your network vibrant over the course of time, or would it eventually wither and die because you couldn't consistently keep up that effort?

What if you said to yourself, "I'm going to connect with one person each day for 100 days?" Assuming you do this every weekday, it will take you 20 weeks, which is just short of 5 months. Thinking about it that way may be overwhelming.

When was the last time you did anything every day for 5 months?

But if you only have to connect with one person, it's probably something you could do in a few minutes each day. When you focus on making the one connection each day, and don't stop, you'll eventually get to 100 contacts.

Don't focus on the 5 months. Focus on what's in front of you today. Do one thing and connect with one person. Tomorrow, do the same thing.

Like the tortoise, don't stop. Eventually, you'll win the race.

John invited me to coffee one morning. I hadn't talked to him in person in almost a year. He was in my coaching group and wanted to grow his professional network slowly, over time. "I can't believe how many new people I've met in the past year," he told me. "I just tried to connect with one person each week. Sometimes it led to something and other times it didn't, but I kept going every week, and I have come across new jobs and volunteer opportunities all year."

John didn't sprint out and contact everyone he knew. He proceeded slowly. He wasn't cautious or hesitant, but he was deliberate. Each week he was connecting with people, and they were connecting him with other people. His network was growing slowly, but it was always expanding.

Now a year later, John felt like he had gone from no network to a vibrant professional network. It took time, but it wasn't difficult. In fact, he was surprised by how easy it was.

Professional networking is going to take time. It's easy to get impatient. It's easy to want it all to happen quickly, but it takes patience. It's slow. You're building relationships with other people, which means from time to time you're going to be waiting for other people to respond to you. You may connect with someone and they don't respond right away. Sometimes people want to think about what to say. In time, they will respond.

Soon, you'll discover you might have more people responding than you have time for. It's a good problem to have and one you can handle by slowing down the rate at which you are connecting. But if you don't keep connecting, you won't have this problem.

Today, reflect on the steps you've learned in this book. Pick one of them. Make the action as tiny as possible. Do the same thing tomorrow. And the next day. And the next day. And the next day...

> *"It does not matter how slowly you go as long as you do not stop."*
> *— Confucius*

CONCLUSION

For introverts, connecting with new people can feel scary or intimidating or difficult. But it is possible to grow a vibrant professional network as an introvert.

As you've seen in the fables, small, consistent actions will help you tap into existing relationships, which will lead to introductions and opportunities. These actions can be accomplished without going to networking events where you must walk into a room full of strangers. You also don't need to send emails or make phone calls to people you don't know. Instead, if you follow the steps in the fables, you'll soon get introduced to new connections, and your professional network will begin to grow.

Let's review what we've learned:

Chapter 1 — The Bundle of Sticks

- We are stronger together. Networking gives you the opportunity to work with another person to make both of you stronger.
- Networking is defined as creating professional relationships with people you know and trust for mutual benefit.
- Even if you aren't searching for a new job, you should network for knowledge and authority, talent, and career insurance.
- Think about the type of opportunities you'd like to find. Who are the people you know who can help you learn more about these opportunities?

Chapter 2 — The Ant and the Grasshopper

- Growing a vibrant professional network takes time. Start today.
- If you encounter resistance to getting started, change your language to change your mindset.
- Spend a small amount of time every day on actions to grow your network.
- Reconnect with past colleagues, engage with new people on social networks, find an organization you are interested in, and connect with its leaders.

Chapter 3 — The Lion and the Mouse

- Everyone knows someone. Friends, family, and former co-workers are a great place to start growing your vibrant professional network.
- Dormant ties are people you have worked with in the past who you have lost touch with. Reconnecting is easier than meeting new people.
- Use LinkedIn or other social media to find dormant ties and begin creating a list of people with whom you can reconnect.
- Send your dormant ties a simple email or a LinkedIn message saying, "I thought of you today and realized we haven't spoken in a while. How have you been?"

Chapter 4 — The Crow and the Pitcher

- Grow your network with consistent, small actions. Over time, these actions will bring you opportunities.
- If you feel like you aren't making progress, remind yourself that the cost of the time and energy you are committing is small, but the payoff could be huge.
- As your dormant ties respond to your emails and messages, turn these online interactions into real-world person-to-person or voice-to-voice conversations.
- In these conversations, ask people about

themselves and listen for opportunities to help them.

Chapter 5 — The Miser and His Gold

- Some people don't like to network because they feel like they are taking advantage of other people.
- Be a person who gives something to the other person in the relationship. This helps overcome the feeling you are taking something from the other person.
- Based on your real-life conversation with your connection, figure out what you can give. You can give advice, recommendations, or an introduction to someone new.
- The best thing about sharing your knowledge and experience is you can share it over and over with all your connections.

Chapter 6 — The Hare Who Had Many Friends

- Focus on the quality of your connections instead of quantity. People will help you if they have a deep, professional relationship with you.
- People want to help, but you need to be easy to help. You can be easy to help by being specific about how people can help you.
- Create a target list of companies or

people to whom you want to be introduced.
- Giving this list to your connections will make it easy for them to help you, which increases your odds of meeting someone new.

Chapter 7 — The Hare and the Tortoise
- Slow and steady wins the race. This is especially true in growing a vibrant professional network.
- Find small actions you can take every day to grow your network. Build a Tiny Habit around these actions.
- Connect with one dormant tie. Send one email or LinkedIn message. Have one real-life conversation.
- Show up every day, take these actions, and your professional network will flourish.

What's next?
In the spirit of connection, I would love to add you to my vibrant professional network.

I'd also love to hear about your struggles and successes growing your network. If you use this approach, please send me an email and tell me the results. You can send your networking stories and questions to **greg@gregsroche.com**.

You can also connect with me through LinkedIn or Twitter. My accounts are listed below:

LinkedIn: **https://www.linkedin.com/in/gregsroche/**

Twitter: **https://twitter.com/gregsroche**

Also, my website, **https://www.gregsroche.com** is where you can find information about me and what I am working on.

Finally, if you enjoyed this book, I would love it if you could leave me a review. It helps other people find this book and helps me get better as an author.

I look forward to connecting,

Greg Roche

ACKNOWLEDGEMENTS

I never wanted to write a book about networking. James Altucher made me do it when he wrote a post about taking ancient texts and combining them with your area of expertise. I picked Aesop's fables and they inspired me to explain my views on networking for introverts using timeless wisdom as a framework. I also never wanted to pitch a book to an agent or publisher, so I decided to self-publish.

Self-publishing is anything but "going it alone." A lot of people helped along the way. I'm sure I'm going to forget someone, but to everyone who had a part of taking this book from idea to reality, I thank you.

Special thanks go out to Mary Grace, who I met through networking and who would meet with me every two weeks to see how I was progressing on each chapter.

To all the people who clicked on my AdWords campaign to test multiple titles and subtitles, I don't know who any of you are, but your clicks helped me pick the title.

To Dave Chesson and his site Kindlepreneur.com, all the great checklists and articles showed me the steps to publish a book. Who knew there were so many little things you need to do?

To Shena Honey Pulido, the artist who designed the cover and was the winner of my book cover contest on 99Designs.com. I received 150 designs from dozens of designers around the world. When I narrowed it down, my network voted on their favorites. The cover I thought I was going to choose was not what my network picked. The people who helped me are too numerous to mention, but you know who you are.

To the team at EBook Launch who found all my errors and helped me fix them.

Of course, thanks to my family, especially my mom and my dad who have always supported me in everything I have ever done. Thanks to my two children, Dylan and Gabby, for being the buckets of joy that you are.

Finally, thanks to my wife, Sarah, who doesn't laugh at me when I have crazy ideas and always goes along for the ride. I love you more every day.

My name is on the cover of the book, but it wouldn't have happened without the help of all these people.

I want to thank everyone who has been a part of the project and who is a part of my network.

GREG ROCHE

ABOUT THE AUTHOR

In 2012, Greg Roche was laid off by an employer he had worked with for almost a decade. He had no professional network and no idea how to start networking. Greg is an introvert and would rather go to the dentist than go to a networking event, so he needed to figure out how to network differently to find a job. Through trial and error, he overcame his introversion and figured out how to network in a non-traditional way: without networking events, cold calls, or spammy emails. His approach to networking led him to new career and business opportunities. Over the next eight years, he showed others his way of networking and his students have used it to find new jobs and new opportunities.

Greg has been working in the world of human resources for more than a decade. In addition to his day job, he always has side projects. He's been a real estate investor, a food truck owner, a franchise owner, a writer, and a speaker. His most important project is his family, which includes his wife, Sarah, and his two children, Dylan and Gabby.

GREG ROCHE

www.ingramcontent.com/pod-product-compliance
Lightning Source LLC
Chambersburg PA
CBHW031925240526
45464CB00022B/898